Mark S. Utterwerk

BEN, THE ADVENTURES OF A HUNTING RETRIEVER

BEN

The Adventures of a Hunting Retriever

by John Troy

"Atta boy Ben, lean into it! Mush, mush!"

The author wishes to acknowledge the following editors and art directors who have used his work, some of which appears in this book by their gracious permission: Duncan Barnes, Managing Editor, FIELD & STREAM; John Randolph, Editor, FLY FISHERMAN; Nicolette Barrie, Assistant Editor, DUCKS UNLIMITED; Marty Sherman Editor, FLYFISHING; Gary Gretter, Art Director, SPORTS AFIELD; Vin Aparano, Senior Editor, OUTDOOR LIFE; Ron Lindner, Publisher, INFISHERMAN; Tom Pero, Editor, TROUT, and, of course, Tom Petrie, Editorial Director, GREAT LAKES SPORTSMAN GROUP.

Published by WILLOW CREEK PRESS
801 Oregon Street, Oshkosh, Wisconsin 54901

Published August 1984

ISBN 0-932558-22-4

CONTENTS

To all the dogs we have ever loved . . .

Sometimes it's hard to believe that Ben is a hunting dog.

"Stop begging!"

"HEEL! HEEL!"

"Loosen your drag, Ben!"

"I figured, heck, why stick him in the kennel when hunting season ended."

"Have a nice day at the office, dear."

"Quick, get a chair against the door — Ben's been skunked!"

"Stop doing walleye pike impressions while we're eating."

"Quite the little begger, isn't he?"

"Why can't you just chew bones for whiter teeth?"

"Isn't it enough I take you hunting!?"

"Hey Ben, wake up . . . psst, Ben . . ."

"It's only a checkup!"

"No kidding, Ben, this feels like a whale!"

"There, not gunshy at all."

"How did you and your new instructor get along!"

"Why don't you develop cabin fever and go out for a run!"

"Is that why they call them booster shots?"

"Talk about your killer instinct."

"I've seen you hunt, why *did I think you could learn to flycast?*"

"Keep it up means your backcast, too!"

"C'mon Ben, time for your booster shots."

"He likes to stay in shape during the off-season."

"Yippee, here we go! Let's hear a little chatter back there, Ben!"

"You can never accuse Ben of not stopping to smell the roses."

"What's the matter, sissy, too cold for you?"

"I said, BOY AM I GLAD YOU SHOWED UP!"

"Never mind who caught it."

"Ben doesn't have much of a paternal instinct."

"Ben's the only one I know that can get 'rapture of the deep' in three feet of water."

"No more Rocky movies for you!"

"He just won't eat the dry stuff."

"He takes me hunting, I take him fishing."

"That's $10.00 for Ben's physical, $7.50 for the rabies shot, $22.50 for the pants, $14.95 for the shirt . . ."

"I said, 'It's time to leave!'"

"You're blocking his sun."

"Ben, give the man his net."

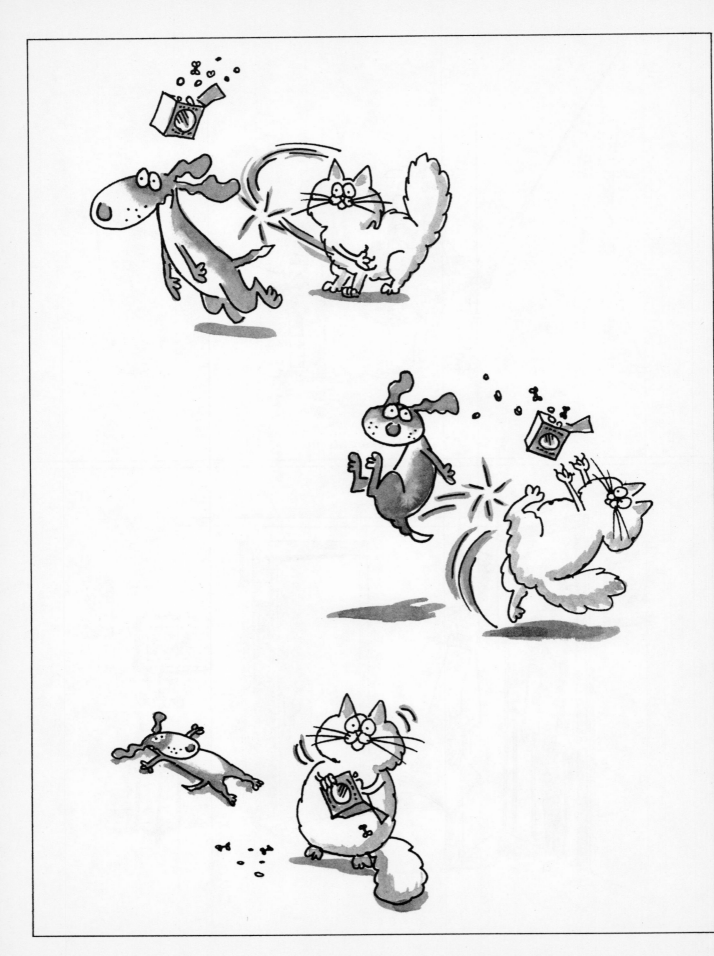

He reads too many cat comics.

"If I hear 'Ahunting We Will Go' one more time I'll scream."

"So what do you think of our new ORV, Ben?"

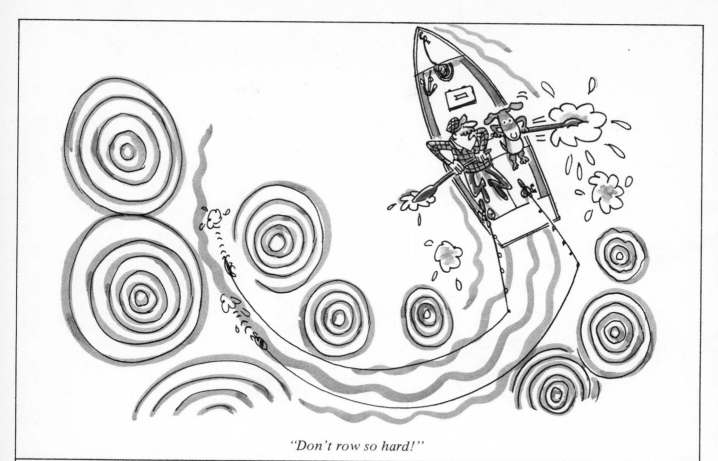

"Don't row so hard!"

"Do you want to be in shape for Opening Day or not?"

"Let's go, we're moving on . . . Ben?"

"Steer 'im over this way, Ben!"

"Do you have to invite everybody?"

"Here Ben, heel . . . c 'mon boy . . . It's a long way home, let's go . . ."

"I'd like to think I've been some influence in your life."

"Ben had his first musky strike — two feet from the boat."

"Number 37, sirloin steak, who's got it?"

"That's it, Ol' Boy, the fire's dying, we'll have to fight our way out! Ben . . . oh Ben . . . ?"

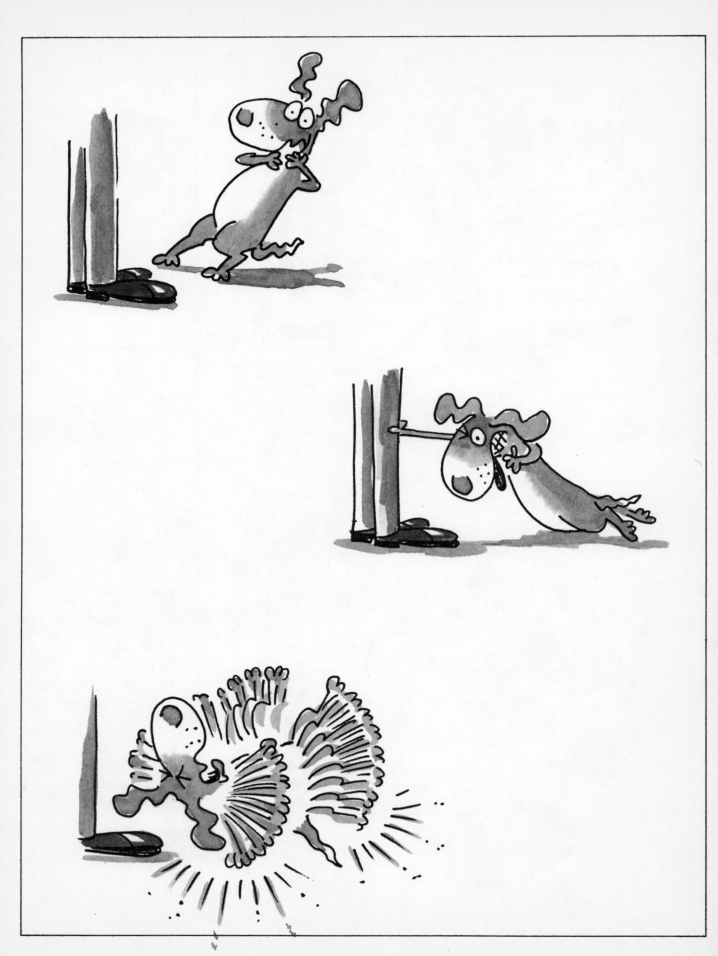

"I don't think Ben cares for this dog food."

"Can't you do anything right!"

"No, no, Ben, you don't retrieve these birds."

"Winning a field trial did wonders for Ben's ego."

"Nothing like a good storm front to perk up fishing, eh Ben?"

"Hey, there's only three beers in this six-pack!"

"Ah, man and faithful companion. Sheer poetry!"

". . . without a moment's hesitation Lassie leaped into the rain swollen river . . ."

"Oh, c'mon Ben, it isn't that bad!"

"Now cut that out!"

"He likes to take a nap after lunch."

". . . and just what do I tell the farmer, Ben, that you, a veteran hunting dog, winner of a state field trial, doesn't know the difference between a pheasant and a chicken . . . is that what I tell him, Ben?"

"Don't look at me, you're the one who forgot the motor."

"Right, Ben, that's three misses — could you run him around again, please?"

"You have to admire his style."

"So that's *why it's taking you so long to retrieve that duck.*"

"No, no . . . wrong bird . . . bring it back . . . don't fetch . . ."

"Ben's not used to ten gauge magnums."

"You can at least look interested!"

"The hiccups should go away by themselves. The grouse, however, presents another problem."

"I know when I miss!"

"Sometimes I wonder about that dog."

"I don't care how many rabbits he found today — OFF!"

"Quite the little comedien, aren't you!"

"Expecting a cold winter?"

"I see it, you're supposed to get it!"

"Sorry, Ben, tall grass."

"Give the nice doggie his bird, Ben."

"Uh-oh, going to be one of those days, huh?"

"Guess who invited what home for Thanksgiving dinner?"

"I knew I forgot something."

"We have a deal — I get three shots, he gets three shots."

"Listen to that hound sing!"

"Ben can't stand wet feet."

"He jogged with me all summer."

"Now cut that out!"

"He's been a different dog since watching the Summer Olympics."

"Ben's having one of his low self-esteem days."

"Now that's class."

"A nice solid point would suffice."

"... Psst ... heel ... heel Ben, psst ..."

"Who wants to go hunting? ... c 'mon boy ..."

Ah, it's great to relax . . .

. . . in a nice warm house . . .

. . . after a tough day in the field . . .

. . . knowing you've done your very best . . .

. . . and earned your master's highest praise.

*Especially when he's gone to the movies
and you've just raided the refrig!*

"So far it's been a rough year."

"No, no, the duck comes to me!"

"It's such a comfort having a dog around for protection."

"Can the comment and get that duck!"

"Oh well, back to obedience school."

"The first retrieve of the season is the hardest."

"Take my word for it, they're easier to retrieve after I shoot!"

"No more watching gymnastics on T.V. for him."

"You talk about your fast circling rabbits!"

"Can't you do anything right?"

"Not much gets by Ben."

"Don't you dare!"

"I take it you got your limit today."

"Ben's not what you would call 'your all weather dog'."

"Aha, so that's *how he gets over the fence."*

"There he goes, boy — trail, trail!"

"Drop me a line when you get to Florida, Ben!"

"He loves fishing but about hunting he's only so-so."

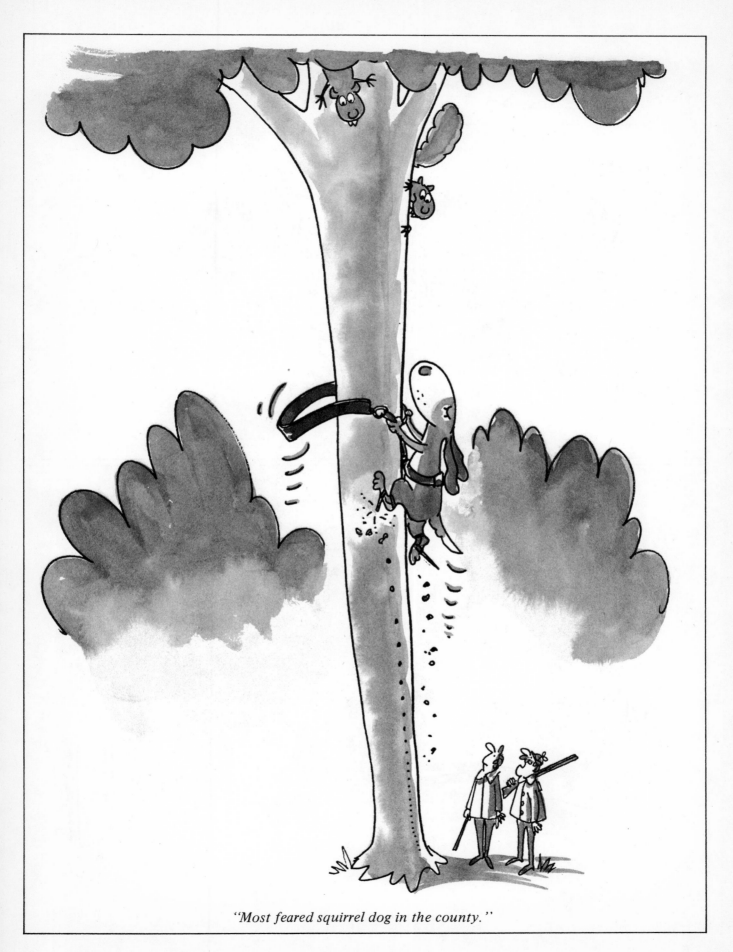

"Most feared squirrel dog in the county."

"*No, no you dummy*, the duck*!*"

"*No, no, you point at the* bird*!*"

"I don't think his heart is in the game."

"A four-strand jumper you're not."

"Oh, Tom was supposed to go hunting with you today? Just a minute, I'll see if he's home."

"Are you going exploring or retrieving a duck?"

"Why do I get the feeling of deja vu?"

"Here they come, Ben, look alive now!"

"Now that hunting season is over, I'd suggest separate vacations."

"BEN, OH, BEN . . . !"

"Any points for feisty?"

"It's a clause in his new hunting contract."

"That was his first hunting season."

"Oh Ben, suppertime!"

"He's been absolutely disconsolate since he found out
from Lorne Green that he's thirty-five years old."

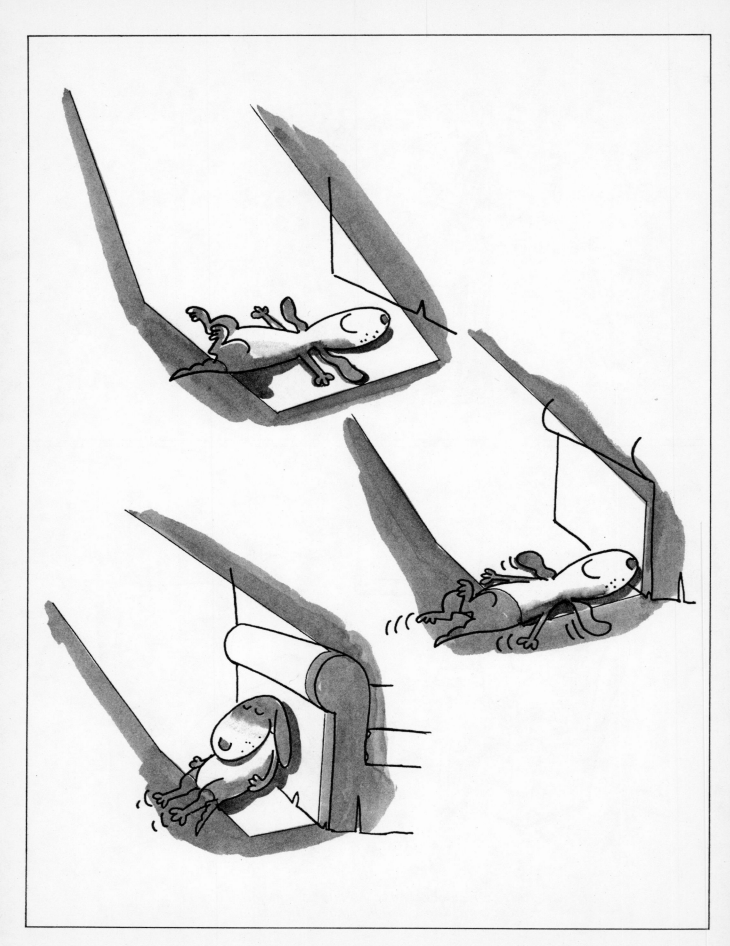

"*I guess that's what they mean by solar energy.*"

"The custom is to fire the gun at midnight, alright, but outside!"

"Never mind the doggie bag, waitress."

"*Modesty is not one of Ben's strong points.*"

"*The note says, 'Happy New Year, boss, please, don't shoot that gun.'*"

I wonder if one yummie is minimum wage?

"Uh-oh, we left the electric can opener plugged in!"

"I don't even have to look, I know Ben is behind this."

"A word of advice while ice fishing, Ben, never step back to admire your catch."

"There, there Ben, the world doesn't begin and end with a fanwing Royal Coachman."

"There's your answer to snowshoe rabbits, a snowshoe Ben!"

"Guess who fell in while we were ice fishing?"

"BEN!"

"That dog knows more darn ways to get around in deep snow."

In this world, it doesn't hurt to have a little confidence.

THE END!